The Evergreen Christmas Tree

WRITTEN BY JIMMY BYRGE

DEDICATION

INTRODUCTION
BY KAT KRAMER

Every once in a while you meet a genuine storyteller. A person who shares their soul through stories, poems and songs. Such is the case with Jimmy Byrge. He is that rare individual , an authentic American voice, that reflects the region from which he is from. Jimmy grew up in the Appalachian forest in East Tennessee , and according to Jimmy he "made these mountains my playground." He felt guided to write "The Evergreen Christmas Tree" which is based on the true story of Frank and Virgie Ann. Jimmy knew this brother and sister, and their Christmas tree journey took place in the 1950's, and yet seems contemporary. The simple story of Frank and Virgie Ann learning the true meaning of Christmas deserves a place among such Christmas classics as "The Gift Of The Magi" by O.

Henry, "A Christmas Memory" by Truman Capote, "The Grinch Who Stole Christmas" by Dr. Seuss, "The 13th Gift" by Joanne Smith, "The Polar Express" by Chris Van Allsberg," "The Best Christmas Pageant Ever" by Barbara Robinson, and the recent storybook Dolly Parton's "Billy The Kid Comes Home For Christmas." It has been referenced that Jimmy Byrge is in the mold of Earl Hamner, creator of "The Waltons", among other classics, who also hailed from the Appalachian Mountains.

As an advocate for the Deaf and Disabilities community, I strive to make sure that each project which I'm involved supports diversity, equity, and inclusion. As an impact producer, I make sure that every project is accessible. "The Evergreen Christmas Tree" is among the first Christmas stories in terms of representation. There's a deaf character named Raymond, an older man who is based on a real person. He teaches sign language to the town, and teaches the reader about the beauty of American Sign Language and the World Sign Language. It's a story with a universal message of hope, love and community. It also raises awareness of the replanting Christmas Tree movement, so important in saving our planet.

Jimmy Byrge is a "modern elder," and this is his first children's book. I can guarantee that upon reading "The Evergreen Christmas Tree" you will be moved. Jimmy has written a timeless tale that is Ageless and Evergreen. No matter what age, gender, race, religion or culture, "The Evergreen Christmas Tree" will be enjoyed in multiple languages, and embraced by future generations.

Katharine "Kat" Kramer
Founder- "Kat Kramer's Films That Change The World" Los Angeles, California

ALL RIGHTS RESERVED.

First published and printed in the United States of America. No part of this book may be used or reproduced in any manner whatsoever without written permission except in the case of brief quotations embodied in critical articles and reviews.

For information address **Book Writing Cube**
651 N Broad St #206 Middletown, DE 19709
302-883-8877

https://www.bookwritingcube.com/

Credits:
Introductions and Afterward - Kat Kramer
Creative Editor and Designer Patricia Riley
Assistant Creative Designer - Andrea Riley
Curriculum Designer - April Hicks

Published by **Book Writing Cube**

Printed in the United States
Copyright © 2024 Jimmy Byrge.

As we ride down the train rails, and see all the evergreen trees, and feel the cold days of winter upon us, I'm reminded of a story that I heard as a small child and I would like to share that with you today.

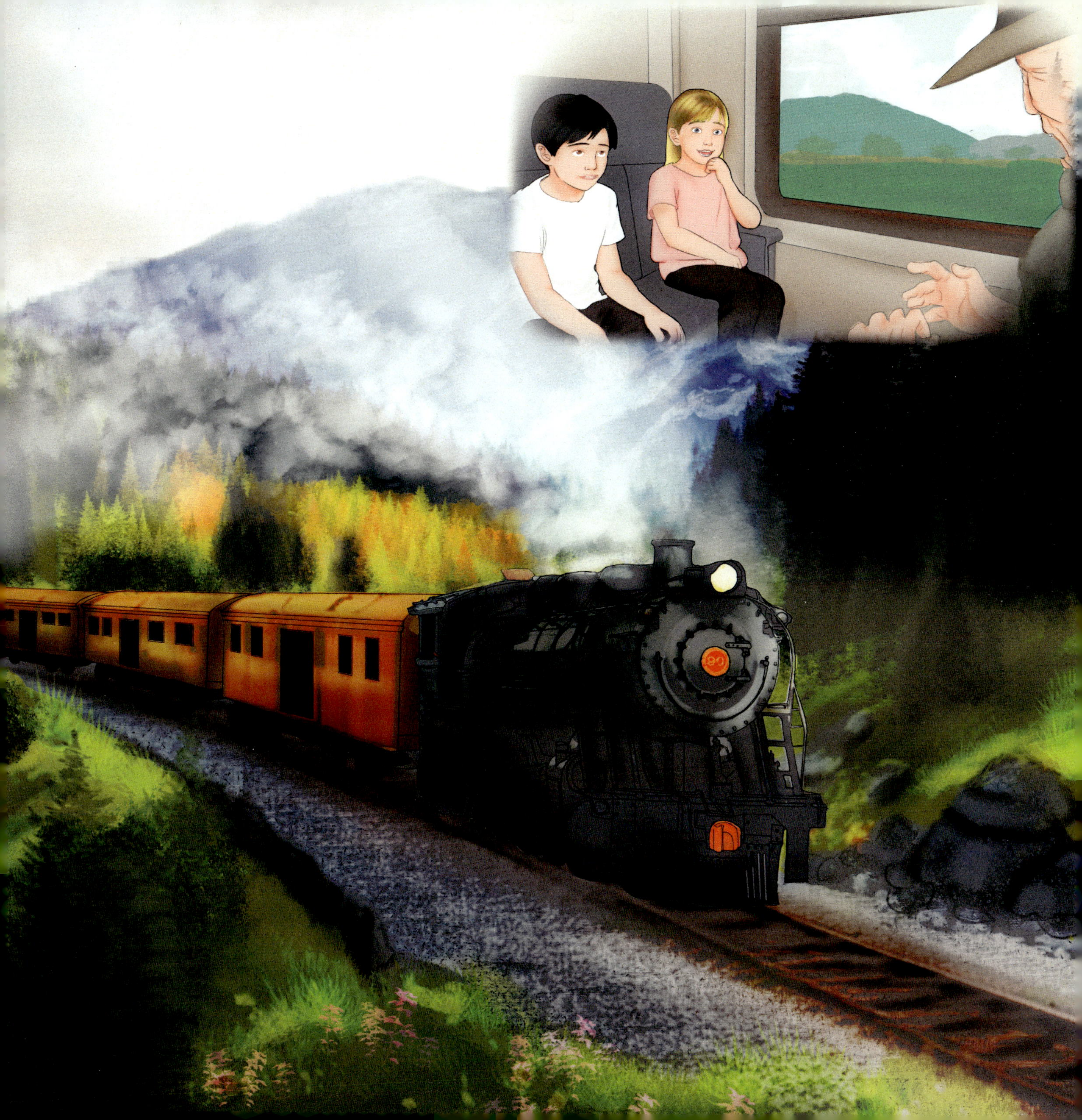

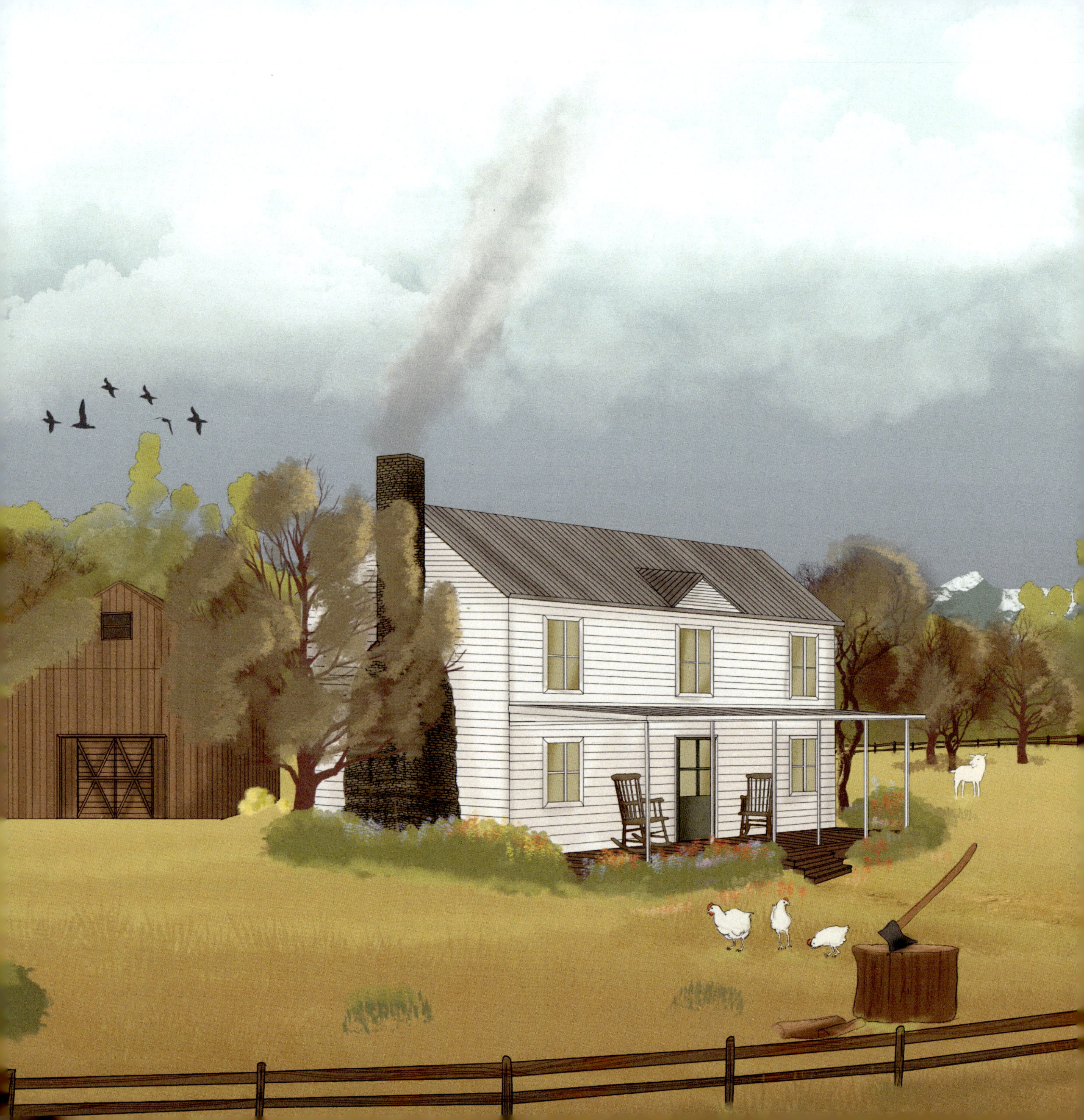

A long time ago, there was an old farmhouse that stood by the road just above Elijah's Fork River, about a quarter of a mile from the train trestle. To look at this old farmhouse, you would not think that there was anything special about it, but I want to take you back in time many years ago when this farmhouse was magical on Christmas morning.

It was a time when there wasn't much money to spread around. Frank and Virgie Ann were looking forward to Christmas, so much so that every day, they would look at the calendar and mark a big red X with a crayon to count down the days.

Now, there were just three more days until Christmas. Their parents knew how important it was for Santa to visit, but they were afraid that Santa would not visit this year. This would be such a disappointment to Frank and Virgie Ann.

With only three days until Christmas, the parents worried about what to do. Father thought maybe now is the time. He said to the children,
"Let's go and find a Christmas tree; not just any Christmas tree, but a special Christmas tree."

Father hitched up Brownie. Brownie was a big brown mule that their father used to plow the fields and pull logs for firewood. During this time, a mule was as important as a tractor is today. The children climbed on Brownie with the help of their father, and off they went looking for that special Christmas tree.

As Brownie took the children up Little Creek Hollow, Frank, who would soon be nine years old, asked his father, "Father, what did you mean when you said it had to be a very special Christmas tree?"

Virgie Ann, who was seven and always had an answer for everything, explained, "Frank, you know we only have a small space beside the fireplace for our tree, so it has to fit just right to go there. Right, Father?"

Father, with a slight grin and the cold wind blowing against his face as he led Brownie up the hollow, said, "I will tell you what makes a Christmas tree very special.

"When you look at a Christmas tree, the first thing you look for is to make sure that the tree is green all over and doesn't have any dead branches. This represents love for mankind year-round and not just part of the time."

As they went a little farther up Little Creek Hollow, the temperature began to drop, and as they looked high into the mountains, they noticed snow starting to fall. So Virgie Ann, being the curious little sister, said, "Father, what else makes a special Christmas tree?"

"Well, I will tell you, the tree has to be upright."
Virgie Ann listened, her eyes open wide, waiting for an explanation. Her father, with a stern look and his face chapped from the wind, went on to tell them that you always have to stand no matter what circumstances you face in life.

Now, by this time, they had already looked at three or four trees, but they were not just right, always having a blemish one way or another, so they kept climbing deeper into the hollow, holding tight to Brownie's mane.

By this time, Frank and Virgie Ann were getting a little hungry, so their father helped them down off old Brownie and they ate the biscuits their mother had wrapped up for them earlier after breakfast. As they ate, they could hear the old steam engine chugging down the tracks with a load of coal, probably heading east to one of the power plants, their father said.

Just then, Frank noticed that snow was beginning to fall, and if you're very quiet, you can hear it hitting the ground all around you. Father said, "We had better start looking for that tree before the snow gets too deep."

Frank and Virgie Ann got back on Brownie, he was almost white from all the snow. They went a little farther, there it was in the distance, the most beautiful Christmas tree they had ever seen, standing just above a waterfall in the head of Little Creek Hollow. They took a moment and stared at the beautiful tree, there it was, as plain as the fallen snow. They could see love, and standing for what is right. This was the greenest, most upright Christmas tree ever.

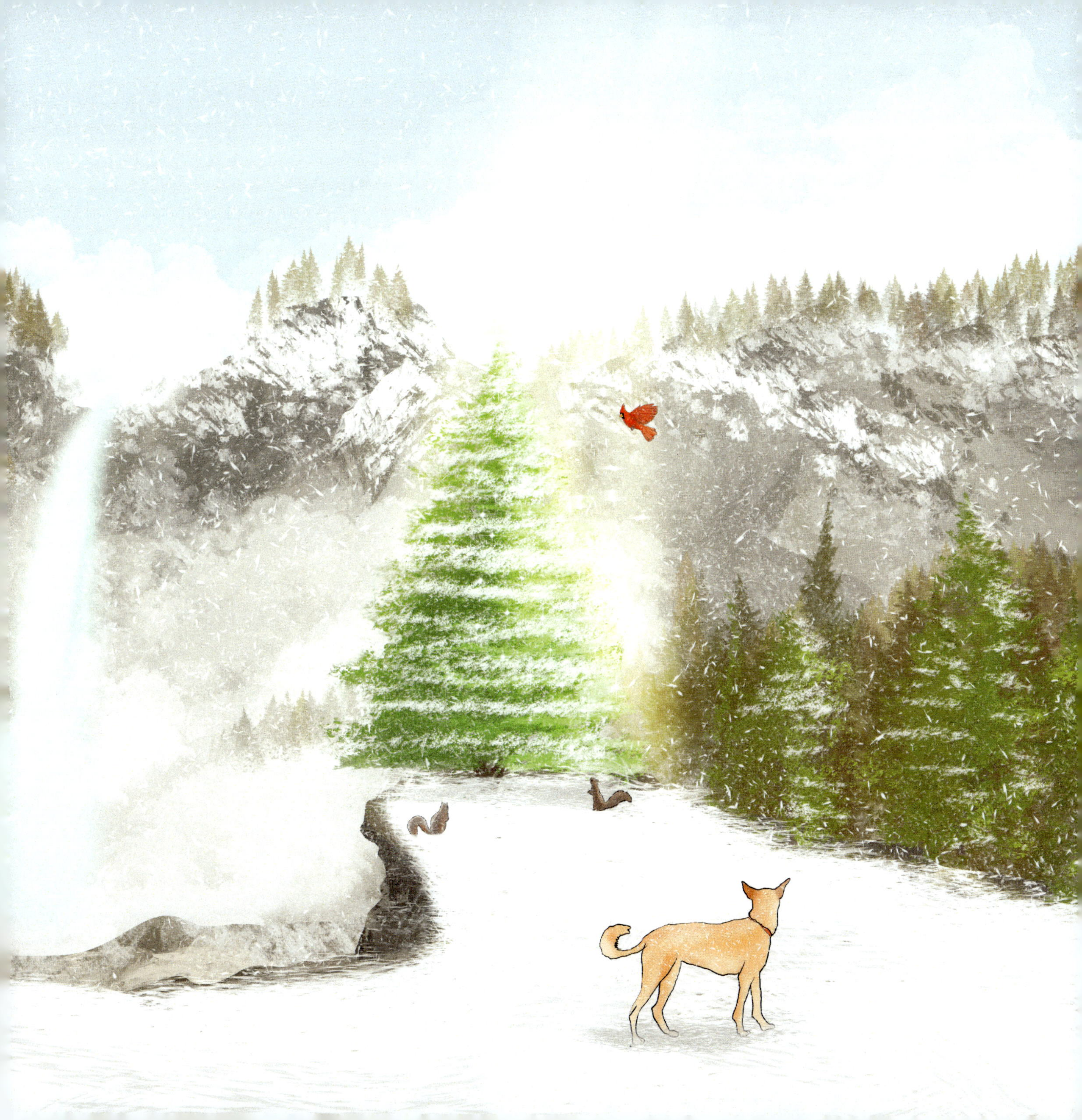

Father began digging the Christmas tree up. Frank and Virgie Ann knew they would remember this day as long as they lived. They took some rope and tied it to the Christmas tree. Then they tied the other end to old Brownie and started their journey back down Little Creek Hollow. By this time, everything was covered by the snow, and the Christmas Spirit was starting to be felt.

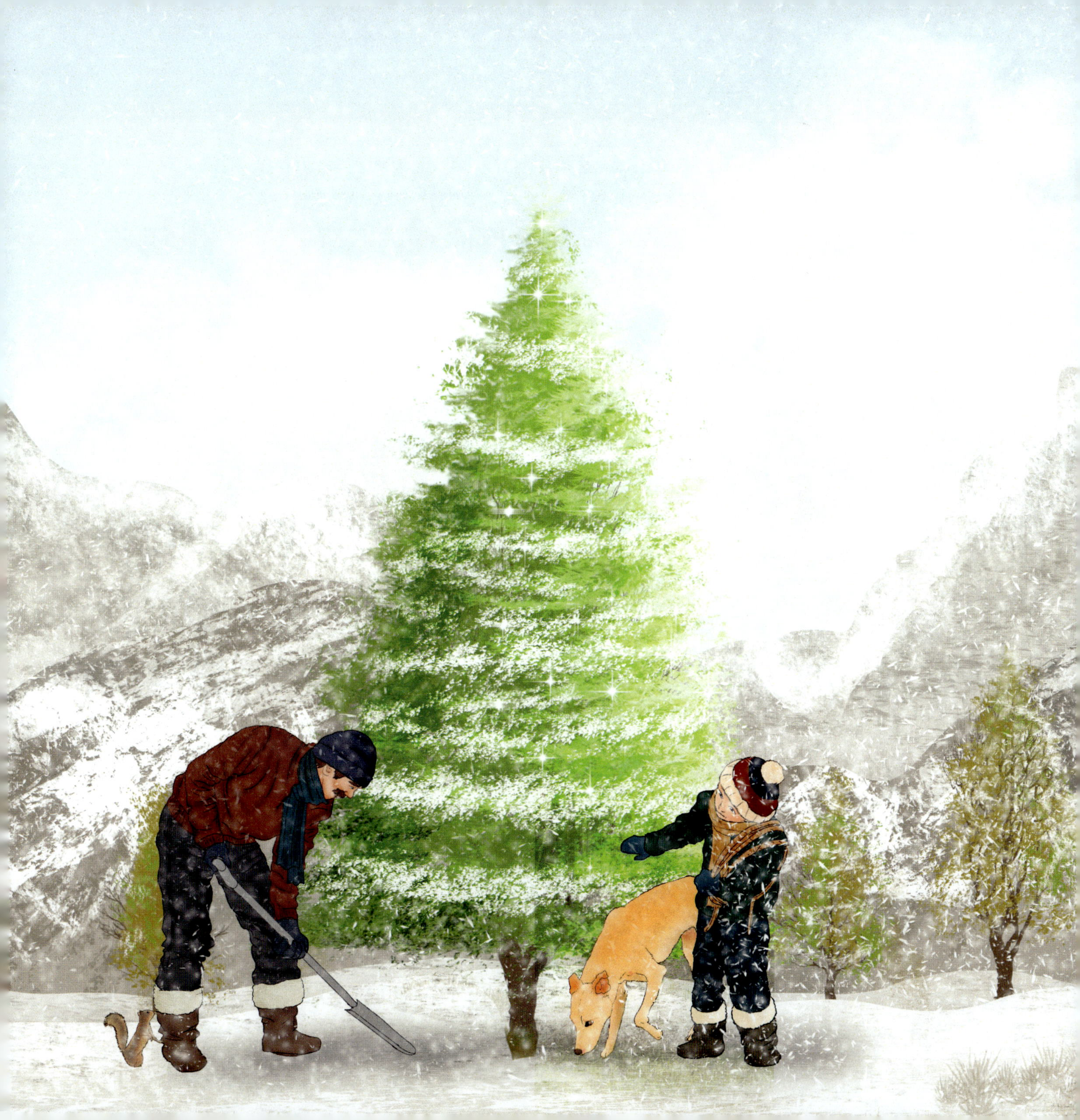

It seemed like no time at all until Brownie was pulling the tree by the old split rail fence, through the wooden gate and right to the front door. You could almost sense that Brownie knew this was a special tree.

Mother came out to meet them as she always did, dressed in her handmade dress and always with her apron on. She took one look at the tree with the snow falling all around and turned to her husband and said with a humble voice, "You told them the meaning of the Christmas tree, didn't you?" Father smiled with tears in his eyes and just nodded as if to say how proud he was of Frank and Virgie Ann. [THEY BELIEVED] They picked the tree up, dusted off the snow and carried it into the house; while their father fed Brownie some oats, brushed him down and closed the barn door.

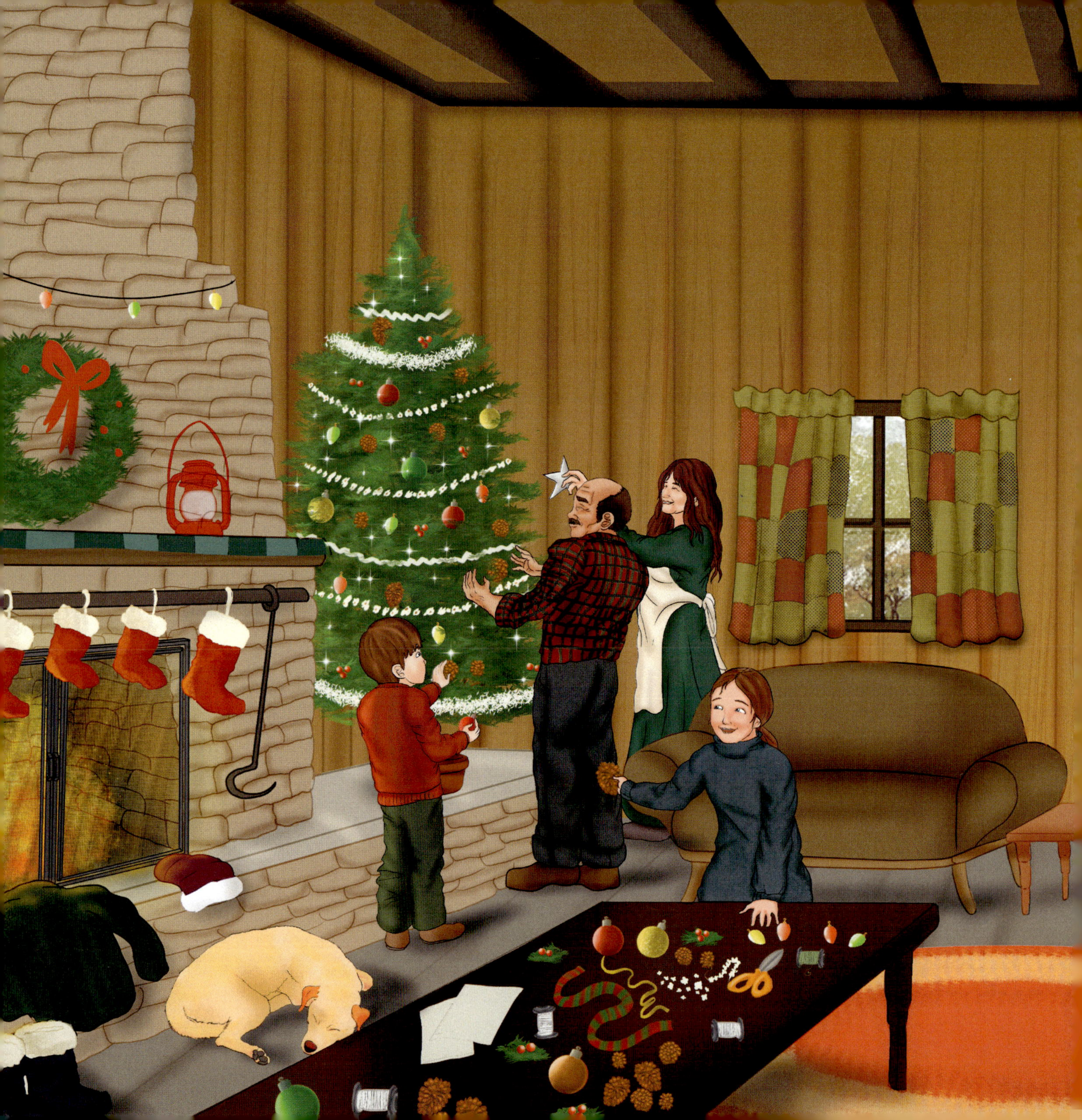

They stood the tree up, it fit in the corner by the fireplace perfectly. "Now we have to decorate the tree," said their mother. So she began popping popcorn, gathering pinecones, scissors and paper and the whole family helped decorate the tree. "Does anyone know what is missing?" asked their mother.

"I know, I know!" shouted Virgie Ann. "The star, that's what's missing!" "You're right," said their mother. So they cut a star out of a cardboard box wrapped it with aluminum foil and put it on top the Christmas tree. "Do you know what the star means?" asked mother. Frank and Virgie Ann shook their heads no, so their mother explained. "The star shines on us to give us strength to help others in time of need." The children knew that NOW this was the perfect Christmas tree!

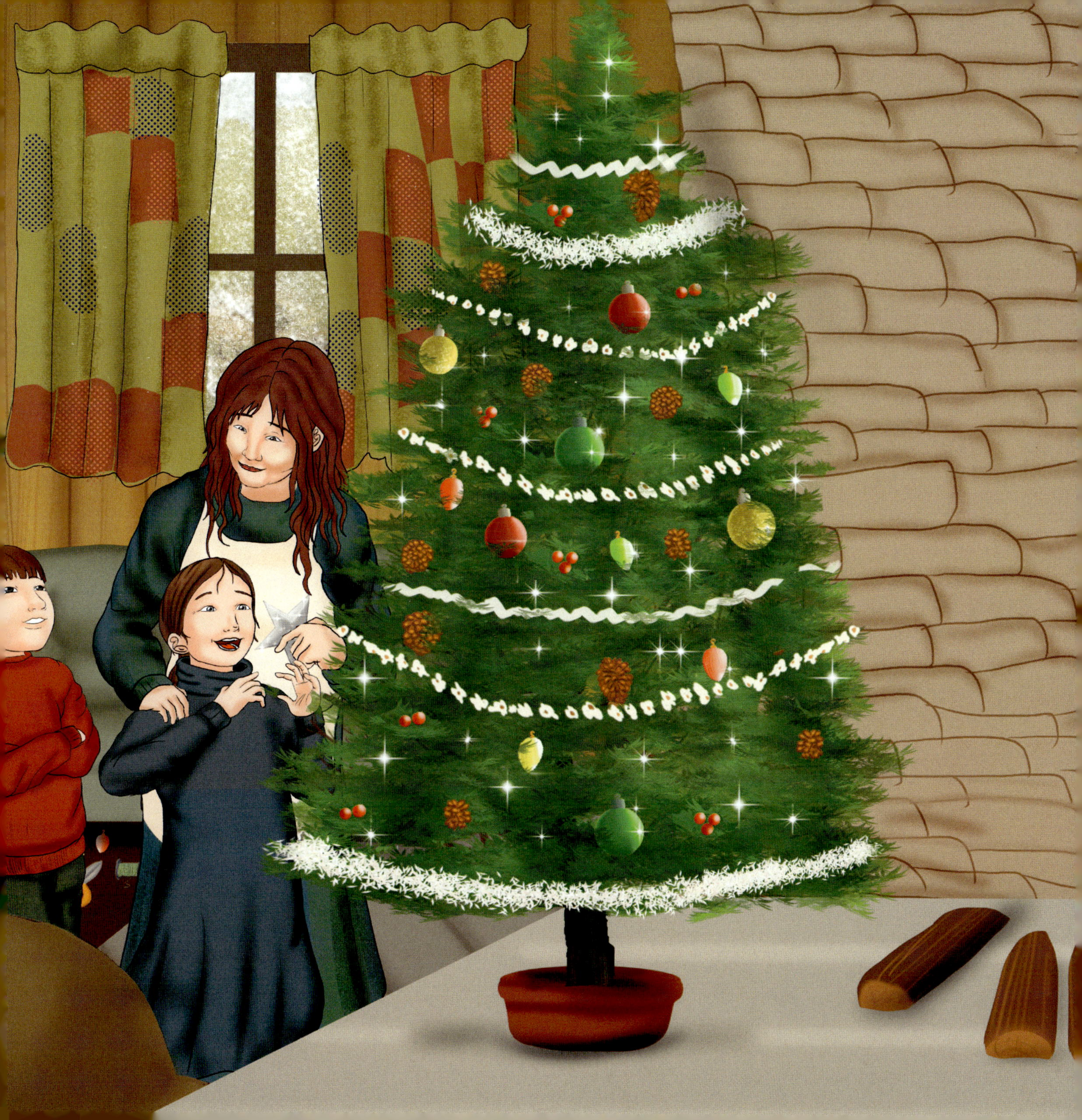

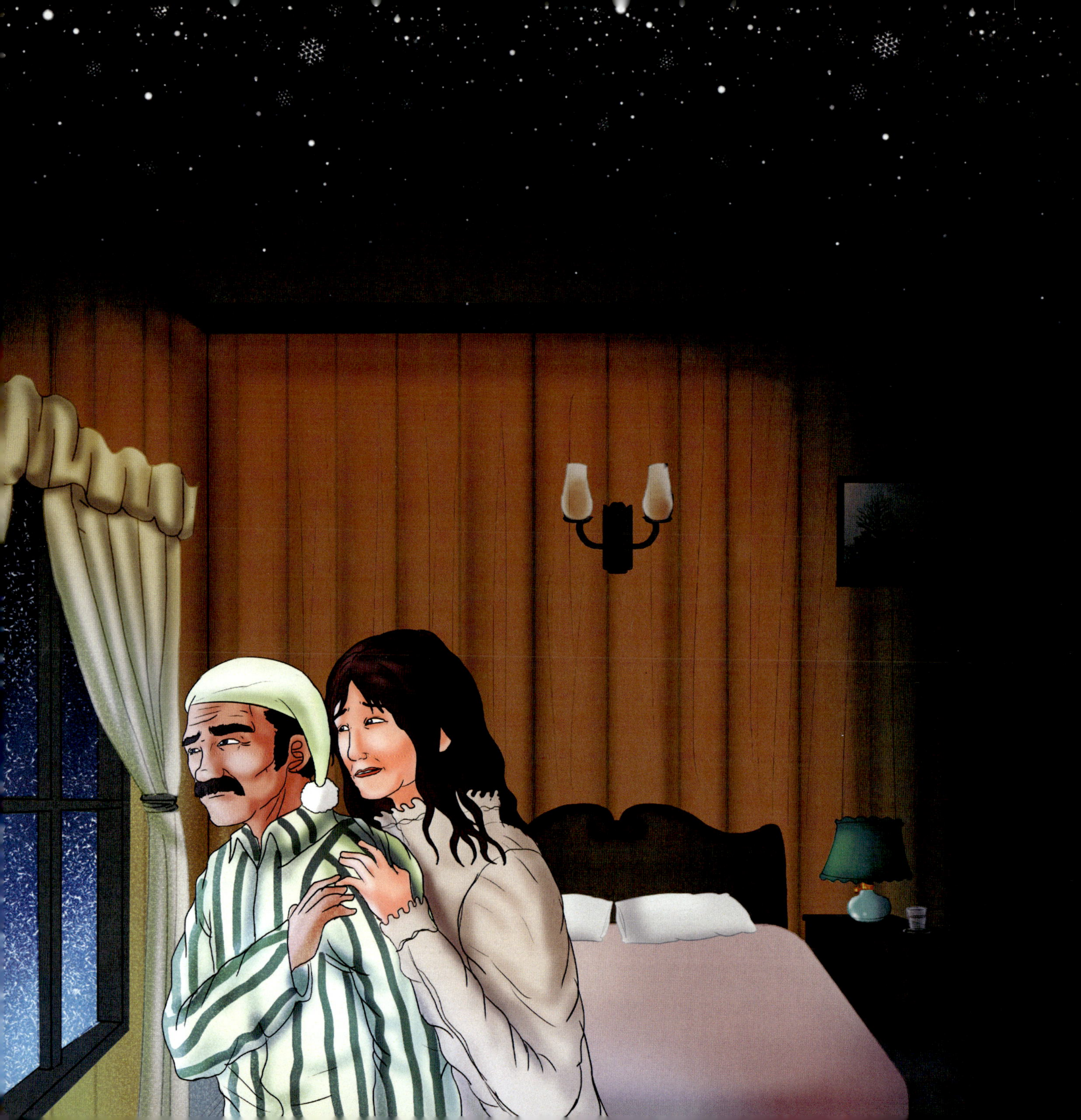

By this time it was late and after the children ate their supper, they went to bed thinking what the day had meant to them. Their father and mother, also ready for bed, were still hopeful that Santa would visit for Christmas, for they knew that they did not have the money to buy presents this year.

The next morning Frank and Virgie Ann were up early and marked another X on the calendar; it was just two more days now. That day, several people passed by the old farmhouse, including their teacher from Rosedale School. As each of them passed by, Frank and Virgie Ann would tell them about what the Christmas tree meant to them. The children walked down to the trestle to where the train dropped the mail and told the conductor of the coal train about the story of the Christmas tree.

December
MON
TUE
WED
THU
FRI
SAT
SUN
1 2 3 4
5 6 7 8 9 10 11
12 13 14 15 16 17 18
19 20 21 22 23
26 27 28 29 30 31

Even Mr. Raymond Wright, who lost his hearing in WWI, came to visit Frank and Virgie Ann. Raymond was the previous owner of Brownie. He would come by from time to time to visit and check on his longtime friend. Raymond plowed fields for everyone in the community every spring, just him and Brownie for many years.

During this time, the whole community learned sign language to communicate with him. When he learned of the special journey the children had taken to get their Christmas tree, he couldn't wait to come by and visit. He taught them the sign for Christmas tree.

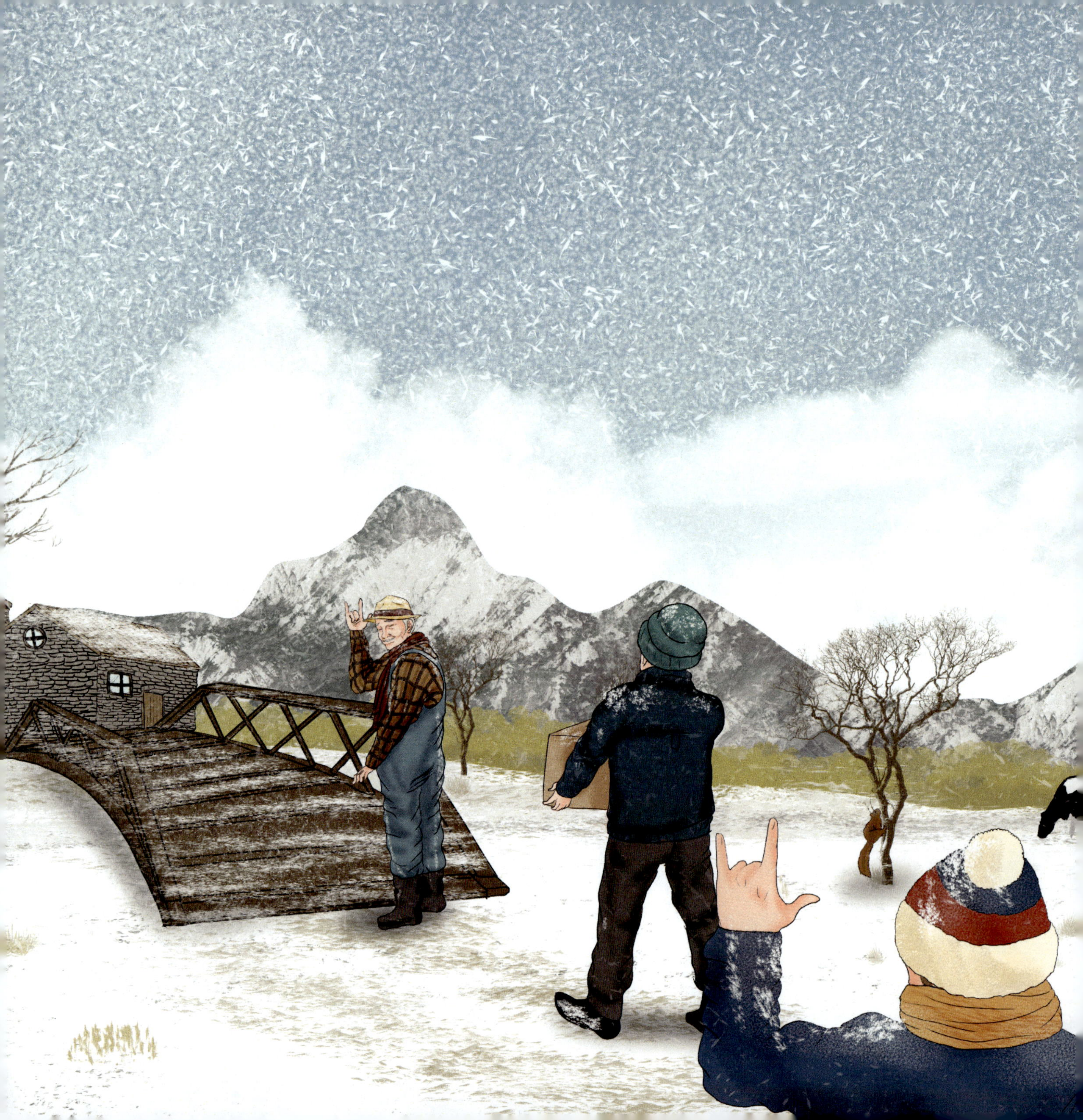

Raymond's visits always warmed the children's hearts. As he made the half mile walk back up the hollow and across his little foot bridge to his old rock house, he reflected on the blessing he received from his visit with the children that day.

The next morning, they rushed down the stairs and marked a big X on Christmas Eve. As they ate their breakfast you could tell they were excited about Christmas being just a few hours away, but the children's parents were as worried as the children were excited. What if Santa didn't come? The children would be so disappointed. Frank and Virgie Ann continued just like the day before telling everyone they saw about their special Christmas tree. How it meant love, standing strong in the tough times, and helping others. Some people cried when they heard what this tree meant; others would just walk away but Frank and Virgie Ann knew it touched them.

As the day went by, the children did all their usual chores and were in bed early on Christmas Eve. Their parents were so worried about how they would explain no presents under this beautiful tree. They hardly slept at all that night.

Early on Christmas morning they heard a shout from the children as they sprang out of bed, ran to the living room, and much to their surprise found that Santa had come. He brought dolls and trains, apples, oranges, even a gift for their father and mother. This had to be the greatest Christmas ever, but how? Could it be that they had shared so much love and good cheer that Santa heard it all the way from the North Pole? That was the only explanation

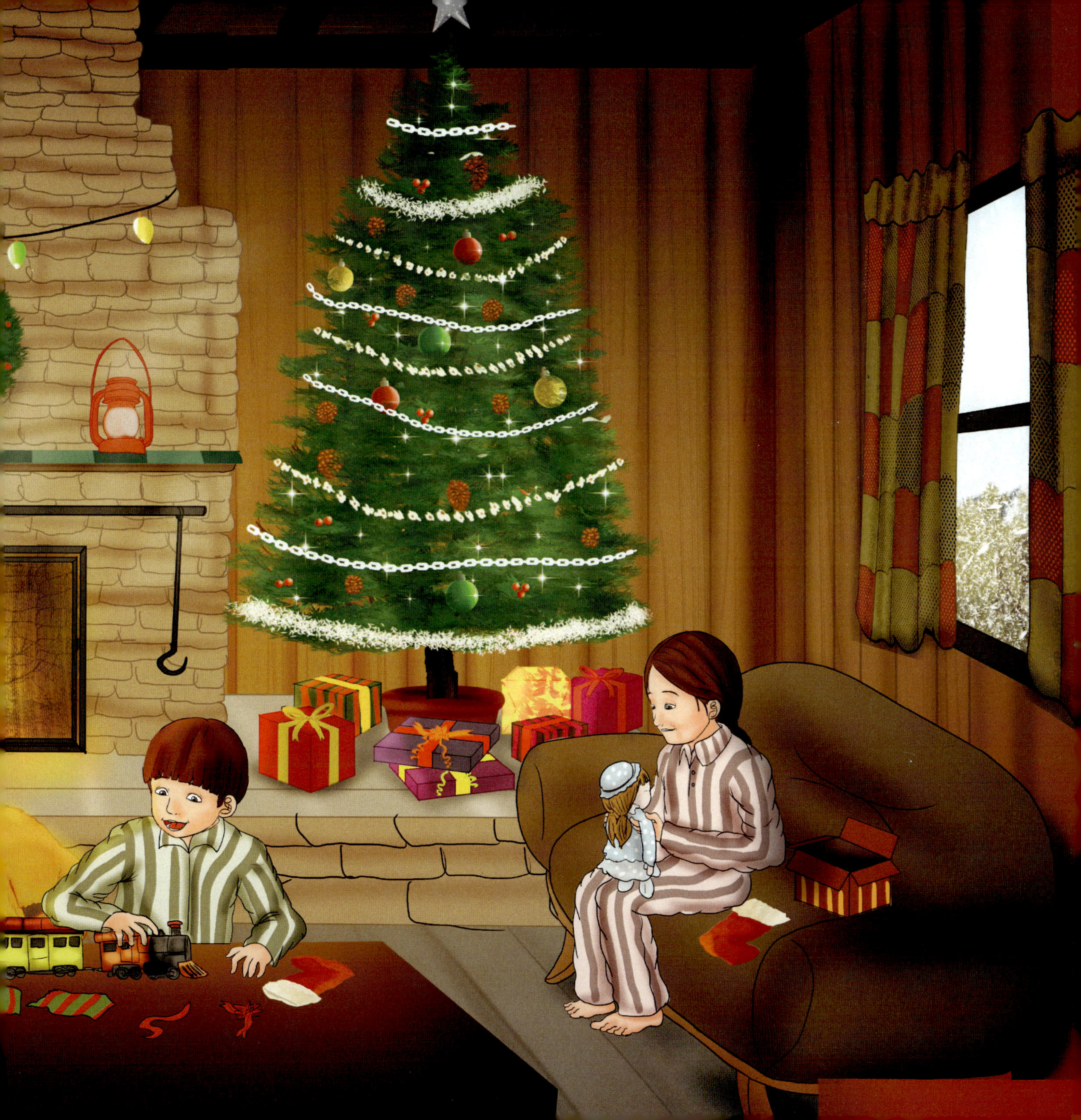

After Christmas, Frank and Virgie Ann replanted the tree in the yard as a reminder of that magical Christmas and the lessons it taught them for the rest of their lives. Frank and Virgie Ann are no longer with us today, but their story still remains in our hearts. Every time I see a Christmas tree, I think of love, standing in hard times, and helping others.

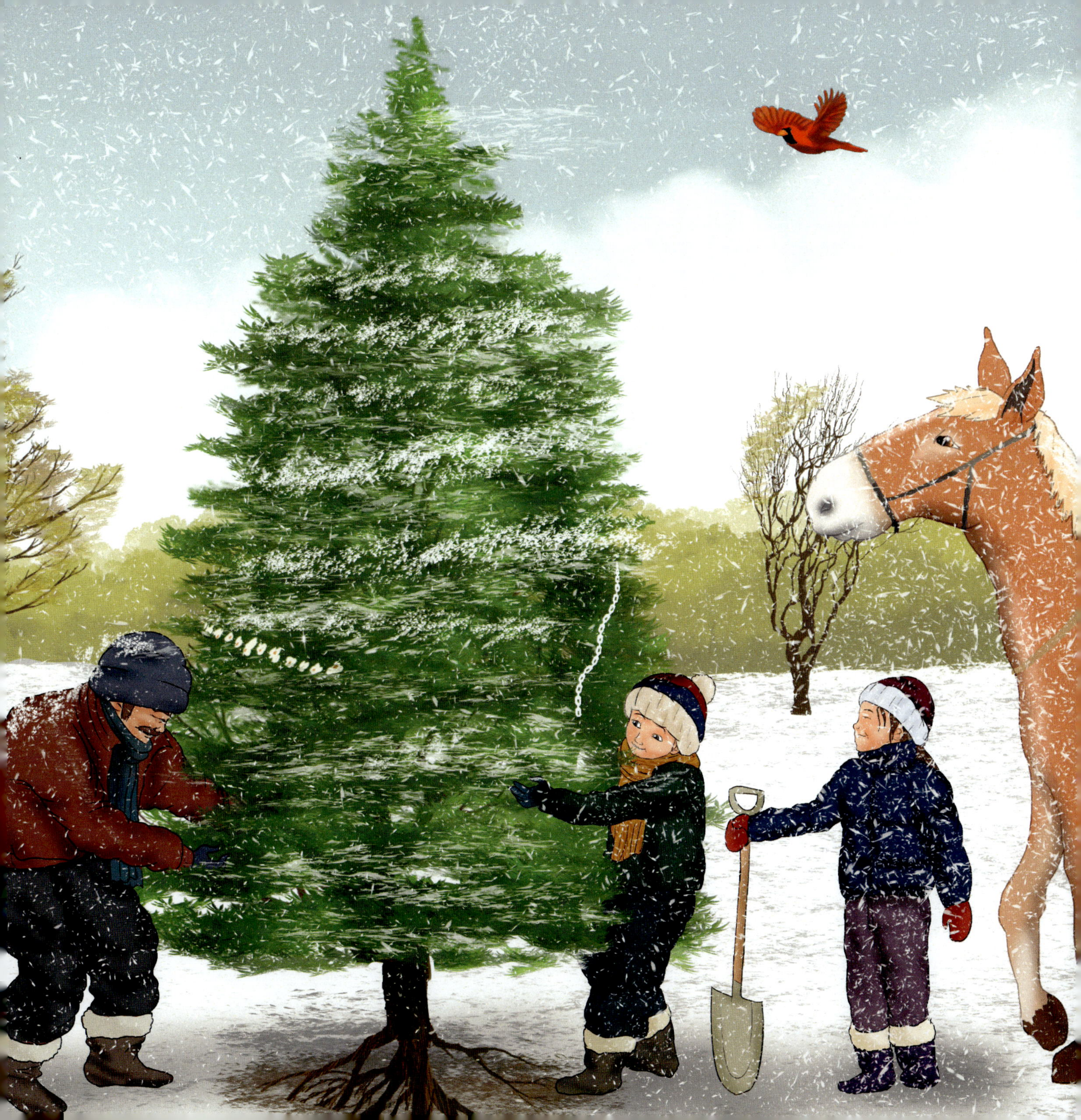

THE EVERGREEN CHRISTMAS TREE
ASL INDEX
PAGE 1

YOU'RE WELCOME	PLEASE	THANK YOU	NO	YES
HELLO	SORRY	HELP	MORE	GOODBYE
EXCUSE ME	SIGN	FINGERSPELL	OKAY	TIME/NOW

THE EVERGREEN CHRISTMAS TREE
ASL INDEX
PAGE 2

MOTHER	FATHER	BABY	FRIEND	BOY
GIRL	WOMAN	MAN	SISTER	BROTHER
GRANDMA	GRANDPA	TEACHER	FAMILY	NEIGHBOR

AFTERWORD BY KAT KRAMER

Well folks, now that you've read and found the magic in "The Evergreen Christmas Tree" it's time to create a sustainable Holiday tradition. Frank and Virgie Ann replant their Christmas tree, and they're setting a great example of how you can be environmentally conscious. It's especially important to Jimmy Byrge that families and our youth take an interest in saving our planet. You can hang on to the Christmas spirit, enhance Holiday memories and help the ecology at the same time. The truth is, you cannot replant a live tree if it's cut. The root ball needs to be intact. You need to spend proper time in selecting a living Christmas Tree. Blue Spruce, Douglas fir, Fraser fir, Norway Spruce, and White Pine are all good choices. It does take maintenance and care year round. Living trees are a wonderful education for children. If you can't plant your tree, consider donating it to local parks departments or environmental organizations as a contribution to your community. If you are serious about replanting a living Christmas Tree, it will transition from indoor tree to outdoor plant. Here are some helpful tips below to keep your tree alive and thriving.

1. Make sure to remove all ornaments.
2. Keep your tree in a cool space away from heat sources. An indoor garage will do.
3. You need to keep your tree well hydrated. Water it daily.
4. Only keep your living Christmas Tree indoors 5-7 days max.
5. Choose an area in your yard with adequate sunlight and drainage before the ground freezes. Your tree must get aclimated to the outdoors.
6. Dig a hole about 2 feet in diameter and 18 inches deep.
7. Store the removed soil in a frost free area.
8. Cover the hole and fill it with leaves for insulation.
9. Remove any wire baskets or burlap from the root ball of the tree. Your tree must be placed in the hole, making sure the root flare is slightly above ground level.
10. Backfill with stored soil, remove air pockets. Water your tree well and help settle the soil.
11. Apply 2-3 inch layer of organic mulch at the base of the tree. The mulch will help your tree retain moisture. Mulch is material that keeps moisture in soil, such as compost, bark mulches, pine needles, shredded leaves and newspapers. Spring is the most opportune time.

If you want to give children the joy of watching trees come to life, there are many national and international non-profits that are dedicated to planting trees.
Arbor Day Foundation: a non-profit organization aimed to inspire the next generations of tree planters.
https://www.arborday.org/

Plant A Tree Nation: A non-profit organization devoted to planting trees around the world.
www.plantatreenation.org

Plant Tomorrow-Reforestation: A non-profit organization planting trees and supporting carbon reducing innovation,
www.planttomorrow.org/trees

Tree People: Born from the efforts of a teen over 50 years ago Tree People inspires and supports the people of SoCal to come together to plant and care for trees.
www.treepeople.org

Alabama Re-Leaf: Making public spaces better. Children help plant trees. Aufa.com

National Forest Foundation: NFF- inspires personal and meaningful connections to national forests across America,
Leading forest conservation efforts. www.nationalforests.org
Plant With Purpose: A tree planting organization celebrating over 50 million trees planted to help end poverty, reforest the earth, restore ecosystems.
www.PlantwithPurpose.org

One Tree Planted: 501 (c) (3) non-profit focused on global reforestation. We Plant Trees! 10 years of impact.
https://onetreeplanted.org/products/plant-trees?utm_source=facebook&utm_medium=social&utm_campaign=plant-trees-for-impact&utm_content=bio

New York Restoration Project:: NYRP believes nature is a fundamental human right. Plant trees, educate children.
www.nyrp.org

Tennessee Environmental Council: Be The Solution- Helping people and communities improve our Environment.
www.tectn.org

Nashville Tree Foundation: The Foundation works to preserve and enhance Nashville's urban forests by planting trees in urban areas.
www.NashvilleTreeFoundation.org

Trees Lexington: A non-profit that plants trees and inspires people to grow a more vibrant community. Ambitious trees planting goals in Kentucky and around the world. http://www.treeslexington.org

Louisville Grows: Growing Greener, Healthier Neighborhoods- Trees and People Coalition: Seattle Parks Foundation-
http://www.louisvillegrows.org

The Greening of Detroit: A non-profit organization focused on enhancing the quality of life for Detroiters by planting trees, advocating for green spaces.
www.greeningofdetroit.com

Reforest Nation: A million trees and counting. Ireland's leading organisation for the establishment of diverse native forests.
https://www.reforestnation.ie/

Neighborhood Forest | Free Trees for Kids Trees for Kids! We give free trees to kids every Earth Day.
https://www.neighborhoodforest.org

Trees for Cities. We are the only charity working at a national and international scale to improve lives by creating greener cities.
https://www.treesforcities.org/

Trees,Water & People: Helping people and the planet
https://treeswaterpeople.org/

Tree France: Your own tree can save the planet- Home - Tree France
https://treefrance.com/

Plant For Future: Preserving existing forests. Plant for the future at schools. Environmental protection means education.
http://www.plantforfuture.org

GreenForestFund: Plant Trees For Life!
http://www.greenforestfund.de

      Once you replant the living tree, it can last forever. Ageless and Evergreen......
       Live your dreams,

      Kat

JIMMY'S THANK YOU
FOR THE EVERGREEN CHRISTMAS TREE

Thank you to
Keith Earl Phillips
Raymond Wright Family

Special Thank You

Myra Phillips Bullock (sister to Frank and Virgie Ann) Thank you for all of your help and encouragement along the way, also for allowing me to write about your wonderful family.

This story was inspired by my dear childhood friends, you will never be forgotten.

Jimmy Byrge

The Evergreen Christmas Tree is very special to me because it was written by my childhood friend, Jimmy, in remembrance of my brother and sister. They were so special to me, and the fact that they inspired this story reminds me they were also special to many others. Jimmy writes from the heart, and this is no exception. This story is the embodiment of Frank and Virgie. They were loving, helpful, and strong in their circumstances. I miss my brother and sister dearly, so thank you, Jimmy, for this trip down memory lane, and thank you for loving them while they were here with us and ever after. Because of you, a piece of them will live forever.

Myra Phillips Bullock

ENDORSEMENT

Exceptional Xmas story. As the story unfolds, the inclusivity of American Sign Language in a children's book shows how signing enhances every and any Season!

Paul Raci

An instant classic. "The Evergreen Christmas Tree" takes me back to my own childhood. A time when the world was a simpler place. It puts us in touch with the values we need to embrace. It's the first Holiday story I've read that advocates for representation and inclusion for the Deaf and Disabilities community at large. I also appreciate the positive message of "save our planet" by replanting Christmas Trees. It promises to be the Christmas book that parents read to their children each Holiday season.

- Karen Sharpe-Kramer, Award winning Actress, Emmy Nominee and Acclaimed Producer.

Scan the QR code to go to our webpage!

Made in United States
Orlando, FL
29 December 2024